BUILT FOR SUCCESS

THE STORY OF

CNN

Published by Creative Paperbacks
P.O. Box 227, Mankato, Minnesota 56002
Creative Paperbacks is an imprint of The Creative Company
www.thecreativecompany.us

DESIGN BY **ZENO DESIGN**
PRODUCTION BY **CHRISTINE VANDERBEEK**
ART DIRECTION BY **RITA MARSHALL**

Printed by Corporate Graphics in the United States of America

PHOTOGRAPHS BY Alamy (Ian Dagnall, Peter Horree),
AP Images (Beth A. Keiser, ASSOCIATED PRESS/MARTY
LEDERHANDLER), Corbis (Patrick Chauvel/Sygma, Douglas
Kirkland, Chris Kleponis/ZUMA, Roger Ressmeyer), Getty
Images (ALI AL-SAADI/AFP, Dennis Brack/Department Of
Defense (DOD)/Time Life Pictures, Frederick M. Brown,
Linda Cataffo/NY Daily News Archive, CNN, Scott J. Ferrell/
Congressional Quarterly, Dario Mitidieri, Time & Life Pictures,
Dirck Halstead//Time Life Pictures, STAN HONDA/AFP, Erik S.
Lesser, Ted Thai//Time Life Pictures), Newscom (Andre Jenny)

LIBRARY OF CONGRESS CATALOGING-IN-PUBLICATION DATA

Gilbert, Sara.
The story of CNN / by Sara Gilbert.
p. cm. — (Built for success)
Summary: A look at the origins, leaders, growth, and innova-
tions of CNN, the cable news channel that was founded in
1980 and today is one of the world's leading 24-hour television
news networks.
Includes bibliographical references and index.
ISBN 978-1-60818-175-9 (hardcover)
ISBN 978-0-89812-760-7 (pbk)
1. Cable News Network—Juvenile literature. 2. Television
broadcasting of news—United States—Juvenile literature.
I. Title. II. Title: Story of Cable News Network.

PN4888.T4G55 2012
070.4'3—dc23   2011035751

First edition

987654321

CREATIVE
PAPER ƧʞƆAꓭ

THE STORY OF

CNN

SARA GILBERT

People around the world were watching the Cable News Network (CNN) on the morning of Tuesday, January 28, 1986, to see the launch of the space shuttle *Challenger*. A television channel devoted entirely to news, CNN was broadcasting the event live from the Kennedy Space Center in Florida. Although the other networks covering the launch cut to commercials about a minute into the shuttle's flight, CNN continued to offer a live picture of the *Challenger* as it rose into the sky. It was the only network still broadcasting when the shuttle burst into flames and smoke 73 seconds after launch, killing everyone on board, including teacher Christa McAuliffe. CNN's 2 anchors covering the event remained on the air for the next 13 hours, solidifying the network's reputation as *the* source for live, breaking news.

CHAPTER ONE

New News

In the fall of 1978, businessman Ted Turner called Reese Schonfeld, a journalist he had met only a few times before. Turner was the owner of the Atlanta Braves baseball team and Turner Broadcasting System (TBS), which operated a cable television station based in Atlanta, Georgia; Schonfeld was a 23-year TV news veteran.

Turner wanted Schonfeld's help launching a 24-hour cable news service that would broadcast live via **satellite** to the whole country and, eventually, to people in countries all across the world. "Can it be done?" Turner asked Schonfeld. "And will you do it with me?"

Schonfeld appreciated Turner's vision of a television network that would put breaking news in front of viewers as it happened, helping them to become better-informed citizens. So in August 1979, he moved to Atlanta and helped Turner create CNN. Schonfeld was tasked with hiring the reporters, anchors, and producers who would create and deliver the content broadcast on CNN. He also worked to set up **bureaus** across the country to deliver local news. Turner, meanwhile, worked to build the necessary financial foundation. He had to round up advertisers to support the venture and convince the owners of cable operations nationwide to **subscribe** to the new network.

Known for his brashness, Ted Turner once said, "[CNN] won't be signing off until the world ends"

Turner's success with TBS and other businesses had made him a wealthy man—but it had also earned him a reputation as an outrageous character who would go to great lengths to get what he wanted. That tenacity served him well leading up to CNN's debut, when money was tight and support for the news service was sometimes hard to come by. Despite a lukewarm response from many potential advertisers, who were unconvinced that viewers would actually watch an all-news channel, Turner was undeterred. He invested most of his own fortune in the venture and, when that wasn't enough, took out loans from business associates.

Together, Turner and Schonfeld restored an old country club in downtown Atlanta to serve as CNN's headquarters, installing seven satellite dishes in the backyard to broadcast the channel's **signal** across the country. They also assembled a respected team of on-air personalities that included longtime CBS **correspondent** Daniel Schorr; Lou Dobbs, who was hired as the chief **economics** reporter and host of the program *Moneyline*; and Bernard Shaw, a relatively unknown political reporter.

On June 1, 1980, Turner addressed the crowd gathered outside the network's headquarters as co-anchors Lois Hart and Dave Walker waited for the cue to begin CNN's first show. The pair opened the broadcast with a friendly "Good evening," then launched into live coverage from the hospital room of Vernon Jordan, a prominent civil rights leader who had been shot while jogging the day before. An hour later, they concluded by saying, "The news will continue for the next hour, and forever."

Over the next few months, CNN's staff worked to iron out technical difficulties and to produce enough content to fill 24 hours' worth of live programming. Turner, meanwhile, camped out in his office day and night trying to make the business work financially. Early CNN employees remember seeing their boss wander into the newsroom to get a cup of coffee in a bathrobe, having spent the night on the bed that tucked into his office wall.

Lou Dobbs became one of the best-known faces of CNN, sitting behind a desk for the network for 28 years

Turner had reason to worry. Although approximately 1.7 million viewers had tuned in for CNN's first week of broadcasting, far fewer watched on a regular basis. The three major broadcast networks—American Broadcasting Company (ABC), Columbia Broadcasting System (CBS), and National Broadcasting Company (NBC)—boasted millions of viewers every day. By contrast, CNN's numbers during its first few years were only in the tens of thousands, in part because the number of homes with access to cable TV was still small. Without strong viewership numbers, the network's reporters sometimes struggled for access to sources and were often looked down upon at news conferences.

Despite those difficulties, Turner remained so committed to the concept that in 1982 he launched a sister channel called CNN2. The new channel ran short, "headline" news stories repeatedly throughout the day. In part, CNN2 was born out of necessity: Turner had learned that ABC was making plans to introduce a 24-hour cable headline news service that spring, and he was determined to beat the broadcasting giant to the punch. CNN2 went live on January 1, 1982, six months before ABC introduced its Satellite News Channel (SNC). CNN2—which was eventually renamed Headline News—benefited from CNN's existing relationship with cable operators as well as the network's round-the-clock structure. SNC survived for only two years before selling to Turner Broadcasting for $25 million.

Early in 1982, CNN was being viewed by enough households to qualify for measurement by the A. C. Nielsen Company, the dominant television rating service in the United States. Nielsen ratings measured the overall size of the audience viewing certain networks as well as the number of people watching specific programs. CNN's rating of 1.1 in the spring of 1982 was still far smaller than the major networks, whose top shows were rated in the 20s—but it was proof that the channel was becoming a credible source for news. Future growth, however, would have to happen without Schonfeld, who was fired when Turner decided that his cofounder had taken too much control of the network.

"At CNN, you were all the way live, and if news happened on your watch, you had better be ready to fly with it."

REYNELDA MUSE, AN EARLY CNN ANCHOR

While most U.S. television networks were based on the coasts, CNN was headquartered in Atlanta

LETTER LOGO

As Ted Turner worked to prepare his new 24-hour, all-news network for launch in 1980, he almost forgot one crucial element: a logo. Days before the launch, he finally hired an Atlanta-based advertising agency to design one. Just 48 hours later, the agency presented a handful of different logos to Turner and the CNN team, including one that showed the network's initials in bold, rounded letters with a cable running through them. That was the one Turner liked the best—and the one that has been seen on screen ever since. Although the logo was tweaked slightly over the years (and was occasionally even animated for special occasions or events), Turner insisted that the design remain constant, even when new logos were suggested. "He put his foot down and said 'absolutely not,'" remembers Toni Dwyer, who worked for the agency that designed the logo in 1980. "That gave me a lot of gratification."

CHAPTER TWO

Breaking Through

Under new president Burt Reinhardt, whom Schonfeld had recruited to join the CNN team in 1980, the difference between CNN and other network news outlets soon became dramatically clear. In 1984, CNN dispatched reporters to both the Democratic and Republican national conventions. The station provided almost round-the-clock coverage of the proceedings, while the major networks were limited to short snippets aired during their morning and evening newscasts.

The next year, when terrorists hijacked an airplane en route to Athens, Greece, and took the crew and passengers hostage, CNN made the painful ordeal available to viewers as it was happening. "Unlike the other networks, CNN's entire business is news," reporter Howard Rosenberg wrote in the *Los Angeles Times* after that event. "There was never a decision to make about when to interrupt regular programming for a hostage update. The hostage story *was* CNN's programming." Then, in 1986, CNN again separated itself from the pack with its continuous coverage of the space shuttle *Challenger* explosion. The network's reputation for thorough,

Starting in 1984, U.S. political conventions proved to be rich opportunities for CNN to draw viewers

live coverage of such disasters led some **pundits** to joke that the letters in its name actually stood for "Crisis News Network." But it also led to widespread acceptance of CNN as a respected source of news.

By 1985, the organization's solid reporting had earned CNN viewers in more than 30 million homes in the U.S. as well as a growing international audience (especially in hotels, where American travelers sought out the familiar news service). It had also helped turn the company's financial fortunes around; after losing approximately $2 million a month for the first few years of its existence, CNN finally turned its first **profit** in 1985.

Perhaps more importantly to Turner and his staff, however, the quality of the reporting had also polished the station's reputation and given it much-needed credibility among both everyday citizens and world leaders. In many major cities throughout Europe, Russia, and even China, CNN became the electronic equivalent of the news services that fed timely information about international events to journalists. In 1987, when Mikhail Gorbachev, the leader of the Soviet Union, met U.S. president Ronald Reagan, 17 CNN correspondents provided continuous coverage of the talks. A reporter from *The Times* of London used the CNN broadcast to write his article for the next morning's newspaper. Even world leaders relied on CNN as an information source. Television sets in the White House, the Pentagon, and the State Department were often tuned to CNN. Both President Reagan and First Lady Nancy Reagan watched the channel regularly to keep up with breaking news and events around the world.

CNN's reputation for reliable reporting was also being supplemented by a broader range of commentators and talk shows covering everything from entertainment to politics. In 1985, Larry King, who had been hosting a successful radio talk show, launched *Larry King Live* on CNN and soon earned wide acclaim for the eclectic mix of politicians, celebrities, and other newsmakers he interviewed on the air. King's program quickly became CNN's highest-rated show.

By 1987, the company had grown so much that its original country club

home was no longer large enough to house the operation. In July, both CNN and Headline News moved into a much larger and more modern office building in downtown Atlanta. The new site was christened the CNN Center. Remarkably, the move was executed without interrupting a single moment of programming, as the signals were officially switched from the old system to the new during a two-minute commercial break on July 13. Employees who had been holding their breath as they stared intently at monitors let out a loud cheer when the signal was back up and running after the commercials ended, with anchors broadcasting from the new location.

By 1989, CNN had 1,600 employees, from reporters and editors to advertising salespeople and administrative assistants, and a budget of approximately $150 million. It was available in 65 countries, from Central America to Japan, Thailand, and Indonesia, and had reached more than 50 million households in the U.S. But it also had its first round-the-clock competitor. NBC launched the Consumer News and Business Channel (CNBC) in April 1989 with several now-departed CNN people in the anchor chairs—including Dave Walker and Lois Hart, who had been CNN's first on-air anchors.

Although CNBC was designed to be driven more by business and financial news than breaking news, Turner still considered the new 24-hour network a threat. The good news was that as CNN approached its 10-year anniversary in 1990, advertising **revenues**, profits, and viewership numbers were all increasing. In 1989, CNN and Headline News combined accounted for 28.4 percent of the national news watched by television viewers in the U.S., compared with 27.5 percent for ABC, 26.2 percent for CBS, and 17.8 percent for NBC. Although CNN's overall ratings numbers still weren't close to those that the major broadcast networks pulled in, the improved market share for news gave Turner confidence that his network could eventually be as big as the other networks. "It'll take a number of years, but that's not so bad," Turner said. "I like being the little guy on the way up."

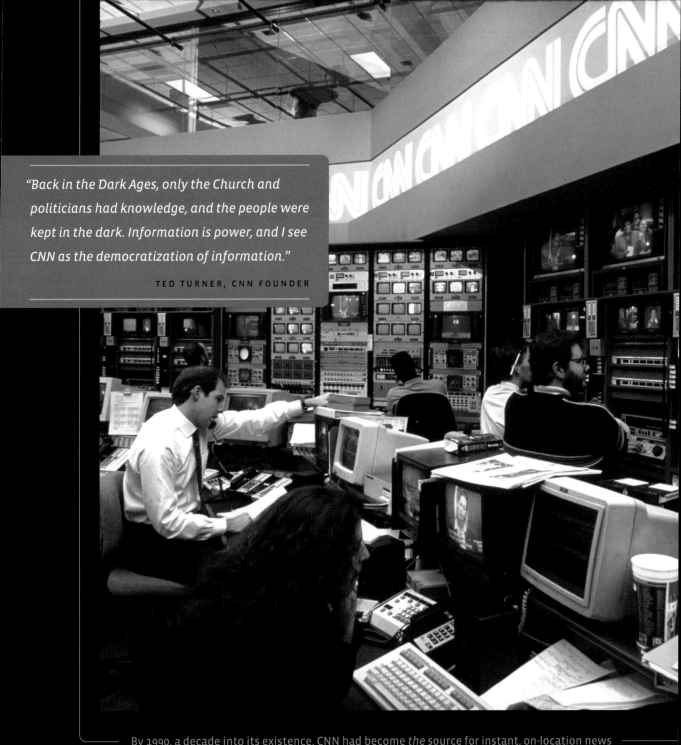

> "Back in the Dark Ages, only the Church and politicians had knowledge, and the people were kept in the dark. Information is power, and I see CNN as the democratization of information."
>
> TED TURNER, CNN FOUNDER

By 1990, a decade into its existence, CNN had become *the* source for instant, on-location news

HOME OF THE NEWS

When Ted Turner was looking for a building to house his new cable news service, he found an old, abandoned country club on Techwood Drive in downtown Atlanta. At one time, the red brick building with white columns along the porch had been a stately mansion, but by the time Turner came upon it in 1979, it had fallen into disrepair. As he and CNN president Reese Schonfeld toured the building, they could see its potential for their company's headquarters. "I could break out the wall, install floor-to-ceiling glass windows, and get some light into the dungeon," Schonfeld said. "Behind the window would be the CNN news room." Schonfeld's plan worked well, but the space quickly became too small for the growing news operation. In 1987, Turner purchased the CNN Center in downtown Atlanta and moved the network into the much newer, 200,000-square-foot (18,580 sq m) home that it has occupied since.

CHAPTER THREE

Boosted by Bombings

Early in CNN's history, Ted Turner made a commitment to covering not just American news but international news as well. That included a 30-minute program each day dedicated to a collection of stories from CNN reporters who lived and worked in a number of different countries around the world.

One of those countries was Iraq, where dictatorial president Saddam Hussein controlled much of the media. When Hussein's army invaded the neighboring country of Kuwait in August 1990, CNN began making preparations to cover unfolding events in the region.

Three reporters—Peter Arnett, Bernard Shaw, and John Holliman—were sent to Iraq. In addition, one of the network's executives recommended that the company invest in a suitcase version of a satellite phone. This portable unit, which was packaged in a case similar in shape and size to a traveler's suitcase, would be able to communicate with the rest of the world via satellite even if bombings knocked out the Iraqi communications system. Although the satellite phone system cost $52,000, its value became clear early in the Persian Gulf War. When American and **allied** forces began bombing Iraq's capital city of Baghdad on January 16, 1991, CNN was the only television network in the world with the satellite capability and reporters

During the Persian Gulf War, CNN crews closely followed U.S. soldiers on the ground in Kuwait and Iraq

in place to continue broadcasting live. CNN's on-location reporters were able to relay eyewitness accounts of the air raid for 17 uninterrupted hours. That night, almost one billion households around the world watched CNN's coverage—the largest audience for a non-sporting event in television history.

U.S. president George H. W. Bush called CNN president Tom Johnson, who had taken the reins of the network in 1990, and asked him to remove his correspondents from Baghdad for their own safety. But Johnson and Turner agreed that the reporters should stay. Soon, reporters from other networks and even government officials were relying on CNN's broadcasts for information about the war. At a press conference following the initial bombing runs, U.S. secretary of defense Richard Cheney and Army general Colin Powell, who advised President Bush about military action as the chairman of the Joint Chiefs of Staff, acknowledged that they were getting much of their information from CNN.

By the time the war ended, CNN had spent more than $22 million covering it. The expense was worth it, as the network's ratings skyrocketed. From January through March, an average of 1,637,000 viewers were tuned in to CNN every 15 minutes (the standard time period used to measure viewership). The network even received accolades from competitors, including esteemed NBC anchor Tom Brokaw, who relied on video from CNN during many of his evening newscasts. At one point, he looked into the camera and said, "CNN used to be the little network that could. They are no longer little."

CNN was hopeful that the viewers it had gained during the war would continue to tune in after the war ended. Unfortunately, that didn't happen. When a **cease-fire** was negotiated at the beginning of March, viewership dropped by almost 80 percent. Although the network posted its best-ever annual rating of 1.2, it had become clear that what viewers wanted most from CNN was continuous, live coverage of major disasters or other significant events.

When CNN celebrated its 15th anniversary in 1995, most of the anchors and reporters who had been with it at the beginning were gone. Although Bernard

CNN reporters set up operations in a Jordan hotel while awaiting the outbreak of war in late 1990

Shaw and Lou Dobbs were both still with CNN, others had been offered better positions and bigger paychecks elsewhere. CNN brought in annual revenues of almost $1 billion in 1995, but the network's primary audience of older, well-educated men didn't resonate with advertisers seeking a younger **demographic**, and growth began to stagnate.

There was more competition, too, as the major networks acknowledged the need to cover breaking news and made an investment in the technology that would allow them to do so. By late 1995, the other networks were planning to introduce their own 24-hour cable news services. NBC partnered with Microsoft to create MSNBC as a direct challenger to CNN, launching the channel early in 1996. Fox, which was owned by media magnate Rupert Murdoch, one of Turner's biggest rivals, had plans to introduce the round-the-clock Fox News Channel that fall. ABC began discussions to create a similar station as well. Even the British Broadcasting Corporation (BBC) intended to roll out a 24-hour news channel by 1997.

CNN and its parent company, TBS, couldn't match the financial resources of those larger networks. Nor did the aging Turner have the same frenetic energy that had once led to his self-appointed nickname of "The Rabbit." So when the CEO of the giant media corporation Time Warner flew to Turner's Montana ranch late in 1995 to discuss a possible **merger** with Turner Broadcasting and all of its holdings—including CNN—Turner quickly accepted the offer. In exchange for 178 million **shares** of Time Warner **stock** (valued at about $7.57 billion at the time), Turner Broadcasting was absorbed by Time Warner, creating the biggest media company in the world. Turner was told that he would remain a key figure in the operations of his companies and that Turner Broadcasting would become one of the central entities within the corporation.

"Whenever I found myself with a box seat on a historic story, the one thing I always strove to do was realize I had a responsibility.... It made me focus even more on ... being fair, being accurate."

BERNARD SHAW, LONGTIME CNN ANCHOR

Political anchorman Bernard Shaw was with CNN until 2001, covering many history-making events

MAN OF THE YEAR

The year 1991 was significant for both CNN and Ted Turner. It was the year that the 11-year-old cable news service became globally known as the premier source of news, thanks to its nonstop coverage of the air raids and ground attack in Iraq during the Persian Gulf War. And for Turner, it was the year that he was recognized for turning his vision of live, international news coverage into reality, as *TIME* magazine named him its Man of the Year. The magazine, which had been bestowing the honor upon an influential person or group since 1927, commended Turner for holding true to his vision even when he was dismissed by some as "crackbrained" and when his company was threatened with bankruptcy. "The very definition of news was rewritten," the article said, "from something that has happened to something that is happening at the very moment you are hearing it."

CHAPTER FOUR

An Era of Change

The new ownership brought in new leadership for CNN in 1997: Rick Kaplan, an Emmy Award-winning producer who had worked for both ABC and CBS during his long career, was asked to take over as president of U.S. news operations. His charge was to improve the network's ratings by freshening up the prime-time programming (between 8:00 and 10:00 P.M.). In addition, he was tasked with boosting the network's viewership numbers.

That challenge was more difficult than ever, now that CNN couldn't claim to be the only 24-hour news station. In an effort to differentiate itself from its growing number of competitors, CNN introduced its first channel in a foreign language— CNN en Español (Spanish)—and then opened a news bureau in Havana, Cuba, where no American news operation had been located since 1969. Although U.S. president Bill Clinton had opened the door for American news organizations to conduct operations out of Cuba despite an official **embargo** on trade with the **communist** country, Cuban leader Fidel Castro granted only CNN permission to do so.

Despite those efforts, CNN's overall ratings did not improve—and neither did

Rick Kaplan's time as president of CNN was short (three years) and marked by controversy.

the prime-time numbers. When Kaplan took over, the network was averaging
970,000 prime-time viewers. In an attempt to attract a wider audience, Kaplan
brought in star anchors and contributors, including former Associated Press reporter John King and political strategist James Carville. He also produced a number of topical news specials and launched *Newsstand*, a news show featuring
longer stories produced in conjunction with *TIME* magazine. Instead of bringing
in viewers, however, these changes just cost the company money. In the case
of *Newsstand*, they also cost CNN some of its credibility when a program ac-
cusing the U.S. Army of using outlawed nerve gas during the Vietnam War was
aired without being verified. Although Kaplan had pushed the piece, known as
"Operation Tailwind," into production, the on-air reporter—esteemed journalist Peter Arnett—was the one who was officially reprimanded for the mistake.

What the network needed most was a big news story to sink its teeth into.
The 1998 revelation of President Clinton's inappropriate relationship with a
White House **intern** gave CNN a brief boost. The president's apologetic speech,
which CNN broadcast live in August, was watched in an estimated 5.4 million
homes. Clinton's January 1999 **impeachment** trial, which was aired on CNN live
from start to finish, also lifted ratings. During its coverage, CNN's average audience numbered about 1.3 million households.

In 2000, as overall viewership averaged only 288,000, Kaplan found himself
out of a job. But he wasn't the only one facing a career crisis. As the company
he had founded turned 20 years old, Ted Turner was told that, following its
merger with Internet company America Online, Time Warner was reorganizing,
and Turner would no longer oversee TBS or CNN. Instead, he was given the title
of senior adviser and asked to accept an almost-powerless position as a vice
chairman on the company's board.

Then, in January 2001, CNN's staff of more than 4,000 people was reduced by
10 percent in an effort to maintain profit expectations. Later in 2001, another
500 editorial employees were offered early retirement packages, a move that

Veteran CNN correspondent Bob Franken (center) broadcast extensively on the Clinton scandal in 1998

eliminated some of the most experienced and respected journalists from CNN's roster and left those remaining worried about job security. International coverage, which had always been one of CNN's strongest selling points, began to suffer as reporters were cut or shuffled around to different areas. Although it continued to be profitable in 2001, CNN's ratings fell by 5 percent. Fox News and MSNBC, meanwhile, both saw their ratings climb substantially—Fox by 132 percent, and MSNBC by 51 percent.

Even the terrorist attacks of September 11, 2001, didn't have the same impact on CNN as such crises had in the past. Turner raced into the CNN newsroom in Atlanta after the first plane hit the World Trade Center towers in New York and was disturbed to discover that, although CNN was covering the disaster live, Headline News had not switched to the breaking news. He immediately "suggested" to CNN chairman Walter Isaacson that both channels cover the news live. CNN was the only American broadcasting company able to broadcast live from Afghanistan in the days following the attack, but even that didn't push it ahead of Fox and MSNBC. Although CNN's ratings went up after "9/11," the most-watched coverage belonged to Fox, which saw its ratings rise by 43 percent. By 2002, Fox News had passed CNN to become the top-ranked 24-hour news channel on television.

By 2003, Ted Turner had grown disillusioned with what had become of the company he had founded. His opinions were no longer given much weight, and his recommendations were rarely carried out. In January, he tendered his resignation to AOL Time Warner and announced that he was moving to Florida—news so big that the *Atlanta Journal-Constitution* put the story on its front page. Although he decided not to speak to reporters, Turner did issue a statement about his resignation. "I have not come to this decision lightly," he wrote. "I am optimistic that the company will be able to move forward and reach its true potential."

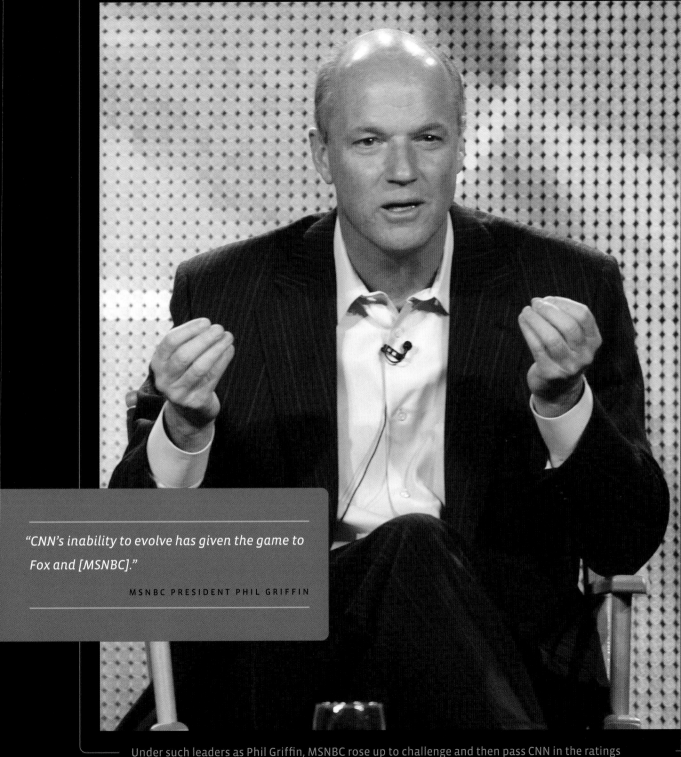

"CNN's inability to evolve has given the game to Fox and [MSNBC]."

MSNBC PRESIDENT PHIL GRIFFIN

Under such leaders as Phil Griffin, MSNBC rose up to challenge and then pass CNN in the ratings

U.S. soldiers in the 1993 Somalia conflict

THE CNN EFFECT

By 2003, more than a billion people worldwide had access to cable
television programming, including
CNN. Many of them, and the leaders
of their countries, were beginning
to feel what became known as "the
CNN effect": the impact of live, 24-
hour television coverage. CNN had
made people better informed about
events—and had made instant access to world news all day and night
a basic necessity for many. But it
had also become an influential de-
cision-making tool for world leaders, many of whom learned about
crises by watching CNN. The CNN
effect was credited for U.S. president Bill Clinton's decision to with-
draw troops from Somalia in 1993
after CNN aired footage of Somalis
dragging a dead American soldier
through the streets after a brief-but-
intense military conflict there. "The
one thing it does is to drive policy-
makers to have a policy position,"
former U.S. secretary of state James
Baker explained. "You are in real-
time mode. You don't have time to
reflect."

CHAPTER FIVE

Bad News

When the Iraq War started in 2003, many media experts expected CNN to rebound and retake the ratings lead from Fox News. CNN had built its reputation on the Persian Gulf War a decade earlier, and it was still considered to be far superior in international news gathering than its competitors. But within the first five days of the war, it was apparent that CNN was losing the battle with Fox.

Fox News averaged 4 million viewers a day, while CNN could claim only 3.6 million. MSNBC came in a distant third, with an average of 1.7 million viewers. "It's a pretty big surprise," admitted Erik Sorenson, president of MSNBC. "People thought CNN would win, at least in the early stages of the war."

CNN's wins had started coming less frequently. Although it was still often able to break news before other networks—including the discovery of Saddam Hussein in a hidden bunker in Iraq in December 2003 and the tsunami disaster in southern Asia in December 2004—CNN had lost its dominance as the primary provider of round-the-clock news. Some blamed political **partisanship** for the abrupt change in viewer habits. Fox News took a largely **conservative** stance on the news, while CNN

ound guilty of
st humanity

CNN kept viewers up to date on dictator Saddam Hussein's 2003 capture, the trial that followed, and his 2006 execution had earned a reputation as a more **liberal** network. Fox News also relied more heavily on commentators and analysts, who were often asked to give their personal opinions about events and issues, than on **objective** reporting by trained journalists, as had been the tradition at CNN. Those differences, some experts said, may have led to the splintering of audiences based on political preferences. But at the same time, CNN's formula had become old and tired in the face of new competition. "What CNN had done to network news—made it look old, irrelevant, pompous—Fox News ... was doing to CNN," wrote journalist Michael Wolff in a *Vanity Fair* article.

Fox was clearly winning the ratings war, but CNN was still ahead of its competition in terms of profits. In 2003, the network reported a profit of approximately $350 million, roughly five times the amount that Fox News was able to make. MSNBC didn't make its first profit until 2004, eight years after launching in 1996. In both 2005 and 2006, CNN recorded double-digit increases in its profit figures. Certainly, cost-cutting measures helped push profits up but so did CNN's diversification—including its strong online presence via the Web site CNN.com and the surging popularity of a more trendy, personality-based Headline News.

Despite its positive profit figures and strong ratings numbers during the 2006 congressional elections, CNN lagged farther and farther behind Fox News as the decade progressed. In 2007, the company announced that it would increase its staff of international correspondents by 10 percent—its largest expansion in coverage outside the U.S. ever. The network also hosted two presidential **primary election** debates, but it still trailed its rival Fox. By 2009, CNN's prime-time programming dropped to fourth place among cable news networks—behind not only Fox but also MSNBC and its own sister station, Headline News. The *Larry King Show* was the only CNN program that wasn't bested by its competitors in its particular time slot.

Even then, however, CNN executives refused to change the network's approach to news reporting. In the face of pressure to mimic Fox's successful

strategy of using hosts known for particular political views, the company is-sued a statement in October 2009: "CNN provides quality journalism. Our rat-ings reflect the news environment more than opinion programming does."

Desperate to make gains in the ratings, Jonathan Klein, president of CNN's U.S. division since 2004, contacted former New York governor Eliot Spitzer, who had been forced out of office after engaging in illegal and scandalous activities. In 2010, Spitzer began to host one of CNN's prime-time shows. At the same time, venerable newsman Larry King retired, ending his 50-plus-year career in broad-casting. When those changes failed to help CNN improve (in fact, the network posted a 41 percent drop in its weekday prime-time ratings) Klein himself was fired, and Spitzer's show was cancelled.

Although the situation seemed dire to many on the outside, CNN officials continued to insist that the 30-year-old network had no plans to implement major changes in its structure or format. The company posted record profits of $500 million in 2009 and showed an increase in 2010 as well. In the midst of widespread news industry layoffs, CNN was hiring staff members. Given those facts, the new company president, Jim Walton, was content to report that small changes to the CNN product were already in the works, but there would be no significant overhaul of the network. "It's not as dire as maybe some people say," Walton said. "I'm not satisfied with the ratings, but I'm not concerned."

Since its debut as the first 24-hour, all-news cable network in 1980, CNN has remained true to its vision of informing and educating the general public by providing round-the-clock news from all corners of the earth. It broke new ground by broadcasting events that no other network could carry live, from the explosion of the space shuttle *Challenger* to the air raids on Baghdad dur-ing the Persian Gulf War in 1991. Although it now faces more competition for viewer attention, CNN remains committed to its purpose: bringing breaking news to viewers around the world.

> "I think CNN is at risk of becoming a bad joke. Late night comics and cartoonists are already using them as a gag line.... It's time for a major change."
>
> REESE SCHONFELD, FORMER CNN PRESIDENT

Larry King with Hillary Clinton

LONG LIVE THE KING

In 2007, Larry King marked his 50th year of broadcasting, including 22 years as the host of *Larry King Live*, the most highly rated show on CNN since it began in 1985. By then, King had conducted more than 40,000 on-air interviews. He had spoken with every U.S. president since Gerald Ford in the 1970s as well as other world leaders such as British prime ministers Margaret Thatcher and Tony Blair and U.S. secretary of state Hillary Clinton. He had conversed with prominent celebrities such as Oprah Winfrey and Billy Graham. In 2010, he even sat down for a rare interview with controversial Iranian president Mahmoud Ahmadinejad. That summer, however, the 76-year-old King decided to retire so that he could "get to the kids' Little League games." Although it was difficult for CNN to replace its best-performing show, in January 2011, *Piers Morgan Tonight*, a talk show hosted by British editor Piers Morgan, took over King's slot.

GLOSSARY

allied joined by an agreement, often military in nature

bankruptcy the state of having no money or other valuable belongings, such as property, or being unable to repay debts

bureaus news-gathering offices located in central or important news centers

cease-fire a formal agreement to suspend military fighting

communist describing a system of government in which all property and industry is owned by the state

conservative favoring traditional views and values or political parties that focus on keeping government involvement small

correspondent someone who contributes news or commentary to a television network, radio station, or publication

demographic a certain segment of the population identified by statistics such as age or income, usually for advertising purposes

economics the study of how goods and wealth are produced, distributed, and consumed within a society

embargo a legal prohibition on the buying or selling of a particular product or of goods from a particular country or organization

impeachment the legal process that takes place after an elected official has been charged with serious misconduct and that can lead to the official's removal from office

intern an advanced student or graduate who works, with supervision, in a professional position to gain experience in a selected field

liberal favoring political reforms or parties that focus on individual rights and the protection of civil and political liberties

merger the combining of two distinct organizations into one through a purchase or a sharing of financial resources

network a radio or television company that produces programs for broadcast

objective based on facts, without being influenced by emotions or personal beliefs

partisanship firm adherence to the beliefs of a particular political party, often excluding ideas from other political parties

primary election a preliminary election in which a political party selects the candidates that will represent it in a principal election

profit the amount of money that a business keeps after subtracting expenses from income

pundits people who give opinions in an authoritative manner, usually through the mass media

revenues the money earned by a company; another word for income

satellite a device designed to orbit Earth and transmit signals, including television signals, back to Earth

shares the equal parts a company may be divided into; shareholders each hold a certain number of shares, or a percentage, of the company

signal a transmitted sound or image that is received by a television or radio

stock shared ownership in a company by many people who buy shares, or portions, of stock, hoping the company will make a profit and the stock value will increase

subscribe to agree to receive a regular service in exchange for a payment

SELECTED BIBLIOGRAPHY

Auletta, Ken. *Media Man: Ted Turner's Improbable Empire.* New York: Atlas Books, 2004.

Rosenthal, Andrew. "The News Media; Watching Cable News Network Grow." Washington Talk, *New York Times*, December 16, 1987.

Schonfeld, Reese. *Me and Ted Against the World: The Unauthorized Story of the Founding of CNN.* New York: Cliff Street, 2001.

Turner Broadcasting System. "Anchors and Reporters: Larry King." CNN.com. http://www.cnn.com/CNN/anchors_reporters/king.larry.html.

Vaughn, Stephen L. *Encyclopedia of American Journalism.* New York: Routledge, 2007.

Whittemore, Hank. *CNN: The Inside Story.* Boston: Little, Brown & Company, 1990.

Wolff, Michael. "The Gray Lady of Cable News." *Vanity Fair*, September 2010.

INDEX